Undoing the Hide's Taut Musculature

poems by

Matthew W. Baker

Finishing Line Press
Georgetown, Kentucky

Undoing the Hide's Taut Musculature

ACKNOWLEDGMENTS

Many thanks to the journals and magazines in which some of these poems—
sometimes in different forms and under different titles—appeared:

Clover: A Literary Rag—"My Mother Watches Me Ride Away" (originally
"Learning How Not to Fall")
The Matador Review—"Birthday Parties"
The Meadow—"My Birth as $f(x)$"
Yemassee Journal—"What the Surgeon General Doesn't Tell You," "Tattoo as
Echo, as Shade."

My immense gratitude to Steve Gehrke and Gailmarie Pahmeier, who were the
most involved with the creation and organization of these poems into book
form. Thanks, too, to Ann Keniston, David Lee, Chris Coake, Jared Stanley,
Dan Morse, and Emily Hobson. Also to the visiting writers at UNR who
helped shape some of my aesthetic over the years: Robert Wrigley, Patricia
Smith, Srikanth Reddy, Chen Chen, and Cathy Linh Che. Of course thanks
to my MFA cohort: Christina Camarena, Justin Williams, AnnElise Hatjakes,
Raluca Balasa, Olivia Soule, Joanne Mallari, Nate Perry, Brian Rowe, Rachel
Chimits, and Molly Gutman. And to Megan Cannella, Casey Bell, Garnet
Sanford, and Logan Seidl, who saw a number of these pieces in earlier drafts.
Of course, much love to my mother, Jill Hampe-Baker, who has been nothing
but supportive of my sometimes lackadaisical journey through life.

Publisher: Leah Maines
Editor: Christen Kincaid
Cover Art and Design: Terry Snead
Author Photo: Jennifer Sande

Printed in the USA on acid-free paper.
Order online: www.finishinglinepress.com
also available on amazon.com

Author inquiries and mail orders:
Finishing Line Press
P. O. Box 1626
Georgetown, Kentucky 40324
U. S. A.

Table of Contents

for Jill Hampe-Baker

My Birth as $f(x)$

I was born to the faux fur of backseats
as water slapped the windshield.
I was born too early and too fast.
In theory, I was born of plates
falling from a balcony, shattering
and glittering, scales from a glass alligator.
I was born to a family of teeth, and the gums
of ourselves held each of us a-gap.
I was born in the same place
my mother was: a bed of steel
and grime, coats of black, smoke
becoming the shape of men.
I was born next to a lake made of geese.
When I was born, cathedral bells rang
and mixed with steam from sewer vents in spring.
I was born pushing at the halogen bulb on the ceiling
of a nursery as if I wanted to blot out its light.
I was blue. I was swaddled. I was born
already moving toward the end
of a tunnel, holding my breath like I was still
submerged. I was born not knowing when
to speak like trying to fill the few silent feet
between driver and passenger.
But I was an afterthought,
as if sprouted from the droppings of a bird
between slabs of sidewalk.
My twinkle in the eyes was a stolen piece of pie,
fat hands uninhibited, taken from someone else's sky.
I stole the opportunity, the whole genetic opera.
When I was born, it wasn't I who cried.
I was born, and then I moved.

My Mother Watches Me Ride Away

Straight street below pedals under small feet
pushing against the old single-speed gear:
my solo flight, finally staying upright.
Wet July air filling and spilling
from my mouth; tongue a tense wad pressed behind
my upper front teeth. But I can't look back
to see her face or hands only forward
toward the bend where I'll have to lean
into the turn, my excitement shifting
straight into fear, my sweat pooling onto
the rubber grips. This dread not slowing down,
nor the bike, and what happens if I fall?
And when I disappear around the corner,
what will she do with her face, with her hands?

But when I disappeared around the bend
I shed my fear and rode for hours
into the hills and over the concrete
slabs of the town. I rode with abandon
up and down winding streets toward a sun
always declining to purple dusk.
Where have you been? she seethed from the car
window, her words like sharpened knives.
I put my bike in the trunk, my body
in the passenger seat. Our ride home silent
as the fall of a tree's final leaf. Dread
rising like a cloud from my sweaty skin.
She squeezed my arm. I turned away. Her palm print
heavy even after she had walked inside.

Birthday Parties

After the third year, my mother stopped asking.

The second year, she wondered
Are you sure?
as if I wasn't sure I didn't want to celebrate:
all the hats and cake and fizzing pop
coursing through my veins and those of kids
who acted like my friends but lately
hadn't been friendly at all. My body ballooning
out, and they, like little pins, poking
fun. Day to day to week—weak,

I started to believe them,
started laughing, too, my meaty
fingers, my sweaty pits stinking
like gasoline and piss not even deodorants could mask—
one after another, sugar, lemon, pine,
even patchouli, musk.
Then powders, then creams to cure
the rashes I'd contracted from mixing
the brands as if my skin was tired

of the farce, wanted out, like the caged
lion at the zoo, solitary, roaring
for its pack, no longer listening to its masters,
refusing to do tricks; the bright mess
of the zookeeper's arm against
the cultivated grasses, the lion stripping
the top skin off almost as if debriding a wound
to reach the better flesh below.

And it was a show
each time I lifted my arms
in my mirror, stripped off sweaty gauze
and pads gone sour over hours, to reveal
what healing had occurred—if
any. The goal smooth white,
but so often mounds of red, ridges
like little Vesuvii spewing forth humiliation.

And what was adolescence but that,
and she didn't seem to know
and so she was
distraught the first year I said no,
asked *What's wrong? Is something the matter?*

I could feel, even then, the inklings
of that change, that laudable bench mark,
as if some horrible wool had just begun
to come off my eyes.

My Mother, In the Grocery Store

She hums Linda Ronstadt behind the cheese counter,

her cut-gloved hands forcing knives
through pounds of cheddar. *Blue bayou, baby.*

Crumbs collect like wildflowers around her:

blues and yellows, spicy reds, smoky
oranges asway in Appalachian breeze.

Saving nickels and dimes til the sun don't shine.

There she bends in her golden years, hip
ossifying in her pelvic girdle,

shoes worn and filled again with gel inserts,

sweat beading and falling from her brow down
onto lips creased deep from years of cigarettes.

Carts clatter past fast then slowly

depending on the busyness of the day. She weighs
and packs. She grins and chuckles at her own

jokes. Past the laughs

she must regret something. I could ask,
but I never have. Now, I don't know if I should—

as though we are stealth submarines circling,

and if I speak, I'll give myself away,
be opened to some new depth

for which there is no map.

She rearranges the display cases
like puzzles—each piece perfectly placed

until it's not—,

talks to herself, scribbles notes on a pad.
Air-conditioning cracks her lips.

I take it back. I don't want to know.

She smiles, waves at customers.
Safer to not engage, to keep her

two-dimensional; easier

to weave her
into a hundred hollow myths.

Months after the Plastic Surgery

my mother moved forward
somehow in retrograde—
her old skin retightened,

bruises, scars all disappeared,
weight sloughed off.
But immediately after: I wheeled

her chair out of the surgeon's office,
fluid filled sacs hanging from her.
Fall bursting in color; leaf-filled gutter.

How easy it would have been to take
a match to them. Quick scrape
across the striking surface, the flash

of flames. I didn't want
to be there, those tubes,
her head lolling left then right

from left-over anesthesia, that form
not of her but something raw
pawing at the wider world.

Later, as she lay there, wisps of breath
issuing from her half-opened mouth,
I measured and emptied her drains.

Her blood pressure ghost-like. Mine
thudding against my arteries. I sat.
I watched. Underneath the bandages

her new body—from ankle
to neck—like thick ropes
of a burn victim's grafted tissue

healing. Almost unrecognizable, this being
who was and was not my mother.
Emerged from this chrysalis

would she be her again
or sleeker, better than?
Or worse? The selfish engine

of my mind revved her into
a million shapes each more intricate
or deformed than the last. I reviled her.

I mourned her. But I did not
celebrate her, who, for years, couldn't
but could now do, for herself,

this thing: rid herself of what
she had, each day in her mirror,
been forced to see.

She freed herself, or tried, and I
could not see that. To me,
her mass was somehow destroyed—

anomalous—and I was the explorer
come back from the abyss—
this artifact in tow.

I Return (My Mother, Asleep on the Couch)

and walk into the living room
to notice she hasn't been listening

at all to my concerns, all terribly
important: the traffic on the parkway,
the sticky summer air, the customer who yelled

I was a thief today for offering him
only twenty-five cents for a ripped copy
of *On the Road*. I could quit,

but there is my need to eat and to leave,
regularly, this house I have lived in
all of my life. Each morning over coffee,

I see the same kitchen wallpaper (dancing
cows chewing flowers in a field),
and each evening—like right now as I stand

over her—the same paintings catching
the orange setting light—one of the Last Supper
(though believers we are not) and one

of two owls (one's back turned and one peering
forward toward the room, toward
what now rises—her chest as she inhales

and I wait to make sure I didn't wake her
with my stomps and gripes).
What if our lives were sleepless

but half as long? She would sell
what she didn't need and travel alone
without a return date. She would

throw herself off mountains and wait
almost too long to pull the parachute
so she could savor that untethered

weightless feeling, the supreme sense of power
over her own fate—don't- or do-pull,
one an ending, the other a resetting

as if once she landed the world somehow
smelled sweeter, she could taste colors, and each
street corner (even in this homely town)

felt unfamiliar. And I…what would I do
having lived without desires or expectations
of myself for so long, coasting

from one day to the next (she
my tether, watching me, waiting
without saying a word) as if the Earth

would spin indefinitely until
I finally made a decision?
But in this life all we can do is dream,

and in her dreams I imagine she is not
alone but a lone traveler who takes long trips
and is free to sit and say nothing.

Though when she wakes, I will say
"traffic" or "work," or I will have gone out
as if I had never come back at all

and she had only just dozed off, safe
and unfazed, the sky filtering closer to dusk.

Body, Burn, Memory

We coast through the dark, headlights cutting
just far enough past the gloom, the wheel under
Sarah's hands—fingers long like stalks—gripping
fast. She slows down for the turn, hand over
hand, leans into it, perfume piercing the gap
between our heads. We both shiver as if
we are baubles disturbed by the slap
of wake from passing speedboats. But rubber slips
on hidden ice, back tires fish-tail out
into the black center, empty as space
between parallel lines. Her face shows doubt
like a limestone wall—sturdy save for thin
cracks between tight lips—as we drift to the curb.
My mind blank, only along for the swerve.

*

My mind blank but along for the swerve, I
pant, unused to high altitude, after
ascending stairs. Just another normal
day. At the top, I peer through the window:
snow piled like the head of just-poured beer
perches on the lips of roofs. Alpine sun
glints and kaleidoscopes off mountain trees.
Winter elided fall, followed August smoke.
Too surreal—my friend's mother's bones, riddled
with tumors, while I take different pictures
of peaks from a stairwell window. What else
should I do? Nothing I say will matter.
I dream the timbre of her mother's last breath
as the next pressure system falls to my depth.

*

When the next pressure system falls to our depth,
it will mix with the sobs of bereft
children. They will have just memorialized
their mother. They won't know how to recover.
They'll linger in the kitchen, over the stove,
cutting casseroles left by sympathizers.
I will offer words, but where do I find them?
Then, over the phone, I will call my own
mother who cannot console me—her body
I picture sinking beneath waves, a black
sea—her tone soft though ineffectual.
She will realize she can't perform her job
completely, distance a hindrance. But,
I can still grieve to her whenever I please.

*

Could I grieve to Sarah as I please?
I have never thought this. On my lips,
her lips are small. Mine need salve,
have calluses from biting dead skin.
We touch, I want to grab her hips, her plaid-
patterned shirt. I want to dissolve her thin
body into my arms. Her arms like wings.
Or, if possible, revise my fingers
in her hair—absurd posturing, dumb feeling.
My body should be a keep of blacked-out
windows. I find it hard to keep steady
my lungs at night, shuddering at shadows
I dream of her on the walls—a haunting.
Did I agree that this is what I wanted?

*

I wanted this; I agreed to sleep
down here, piling blankets to pad my hips
from the cold floor. *I like firm surfaces.* Or
I can't be bothered to buy a mattress. Or
*why should I settle for what I can live with-
out?* Streetlamps glare through the plastic blinds.
I try to think less. When the alarm clock starts,
the vibration shifts it off the table
spilling onto the hard wood. I collect
the layers of my nightmare: her hair
wrapped around my arms, the pyramid
of her torso in the red gel of morning.
My anxieties circulate. I struggle
to remember why I ever said yes.

*

I remember why I said yes: I touched
her lips with mine, felt the small hairs on her arms
for the first time, the moon shine liquid
like boiling metal; veins about to melt,
but a sweet rush, my brain uninhibited
as naked children in a tub. Geese a-flight
in the thaw of morning, fleeing at the sight
of me, my feet cracking on the city
pavement, a march toward doom. What I mean
is that I fear feeling and losing
myself. Being subsumed. But how can I
resist this inner pulse, this animal
magnetism? The length of Sarah's neck
sways like a slow-swinging axe: *Now hush.*

*

Like a slow-swinging axe, the lid begins
to cut off our view of her eyes, her
lips, hot-rod red, her dress paisley and about
to forever collect the ash of her
decay. You said, friend, beneath your thick shades and
wide hat, your mother looked lovely by the shacks
on the lake's beach. I remember swarming
flies above wet trash, peering crazily
over the cliff's edge into the ravine.
I try to sympathize with your narrative.
The band starts up, guitar strings glisten,
percussion pervades the small viewing room,
people sigh and sniff in time, hands positioned,
coffin borne out, palling its way to her tomb.

                    *

After the coffin's borne to the tomb, I dream:
a great lake and on it surfers, faceless,
beckon me to join. The waves rise, shapeless,
fish leap and disappear, water parts to scream,
"Wake up!" I do. In this mild winter, leaves
refuse to fall. Around the grave, branches fan
us, the casket lowers, my fingers link, eyes
scan the crowd. The priest mentions another
kingdom. The sheaves of the pulleys squeak.
Why inter the body if the soul rises?
The ground not a cage but a vacuum sucking
back what it can't bear to lose. At the motel,
the lobby's nicotine-stained walls glow.
We take the stairs, heads fixed on our shoes.

                    *

As I walk up the stairs, head fixed on my shoes,
I picture my mother as modern
architecture: chrome rods for legs reflect light
like mirrors, a sheath of carbon protects
her organs. Her smile, glass. Her arms, flues
though she has quit smoking. Prefectures
of black, white, and red (for contrast) pulled tight
together for hair. Eyes—concentric rings
of dark wood, concave, deepening inch by inch.
She is a glorified golem who flinches
at nothing and devours the weak. I pray
to her—I do—so that her sharp teeth
won't flay my skin; that she'll live forever.
Teach me how to be good—I'll learn, I swear.

*

I swear I'll learn to be good to her.
That night in the car, Sarah's body, her hair
as black as the road, I wanted to consume
her, my hands like hungry ghosts pleading
for skin. I wanted to understand
a form apart from mine, to clear myself
of doubt. But this fear of starting something
outside myself. Branches sway with the weight
of snow. I see them bend and want to bend
like that to whatever end there is with her.
I already know how to be alone.
Lift me by the arms, break me into pieces.
I want to become more than petrified bone
peering through a blizzard, filled with regret.

*

I peer, with unwanted regret, through blizzard.
Today, the snow has reached a record deepness,
and into it will fall pets off their leashes,
maybe children. I am sad for reasons
I understand. Food tastes dry like chalk.
Birds click their beaks, ruffle their tail feathers
on the other side of my window. I hope
souls go somewhere, but I won't allow myself
to utter this in public. I know
the body's stillness means my friend's mother
is gone, no more laughter echoing
through beer season at the lake. I keep
a straight face. Alone, I hope her essence sears
the black sky white, seals up all the empty holes.

*

If I seal up all the empty holes,
will my mother never die? Will I be spared
weak-armed hugs of unknowns, the puffed shoulder
pads of her ex-lovers in ill-fitting suits?
In her youth, she could sit on her hair.
After fifty years, it's still red by the grace
of chemicals. Sometimes I want her laugh,
but space divides us now, great plains, mountains.
Her hip's old, she phoned. She promised to visit
before surgery. I thought, *come quickly.*
Yet I know I would tire of her
just as fast. So what does our version
of permanence look like? Not holy fire,
but simpler, just a stretched-out arc of time.

*

This arc. This time. How to stretch it as thin
as wind without it breaking? Dig a trench.
Plow our hands through the earth, pile the dirt
high like totems. To fortify her against
that ailing hip. To refine my keep
against elements blown toward me here
from the sea—the exterior held at bay.
Now, I cancel plans—I've never driven
through alpine snow, and along the highway
the homeless city made of cardboard
taunts me. Those people fade like memories
of childhood. That type of oblivion
scares me. The gray of eroding gravestones,
the mounded quiet of the green hill.

*

The quiet and the green hills amount to what
I'd like to give Sarah, or imagine
I would. Freight trains chug past at night: caravans
of oil, coal nestled in metal spoiled
by wind, rain, and years. What if they kept going,
rolled off the tracks, slid into the Pacific
like they had no ties to solid ground?
They would sink. Oil slick the only
remnant of their life above, a thickening
bloom of blackened rainbow. Sludge we won't escape.
Our fall forecasted, written in my genes.
Trapped, failed, this fear of intimacy rising
if only I could—Stop. Listen to the whine
under hot stars as train wheels grind the dust.

*

Under playa stars, train wheels grind the dust
into a storm. I have collected the bones
of the women of my life, have erected
monuments in me. They flash brighter
than anything celestial in this
wasteland. Burn my body in their memory:
Sarah behind the steering wheel; a mother
and her cancer and her daughter, my friend;
the red of my mother graying at the roots.
My head filled. Today I found the last
message I exchanged with that friend's dying
mother. She sent me all her love and peace.
I want to speed out into the desert's gloom,
cut the headlights, coast with us all through the dark.

Finding the New World

Her hip beneath the sea
of her blood waits

for the knife's sterilized edge.
She fears the loss

of her former self, her de-
construction. The nurse numbs her lower half,

and like a magician's assistant
she is split

at the pelvis. Her brain disconnected
from its lower self

floats in the new whole
of its upper. Awake, she watches

her legs glide free from sensation.
The blade cuts in, the skin peels back.

And though she sees the carnage of herself
laid open, she realizes the body

is a neutral zone tethered
to pain unwillingly. She wishes

she could remain
in that fog, that

blankness between delivery
and receipt. The surgeon scoops

the pearl-white mass of bone
from the well of her leg, rejoins

her muscle fibers to a bright
titanium ball and socket.

In this moment she wishes
to peer into herself and see

the mechanism of her body pulsing,
to discover the inward layers

of herself no longer hidden but
clear—her cut

a glass surface. She beholds
a landscape she's never been able to reach.

Though what unnerves her now is
not the bloodied gauze

petaled around her, not her altered
mass, but her cold fascination

as if now that she's detached
from her body it has become

this new country and she is its
conquistador. Its interior

is dense—an uncut jungle
her mind demands she map.

But what if, after she begins
to descend into the maze

of herself, she finds no center,
no whole to piece together;

realizes to be whole was always an illusion,
that, when she comes to

in the bright white hospital room, the pain
will return, too, as if

it had never left, each nerve
broken and aflame.

What the Surgeon General Doesn't Tell You

The years have been kind
and cruel to your suite
of moss-darkened curves—
lungs blackened by smoke you took in,
but not born that way. Rosy, at first,
like your sister's flushed cheeks
when she chased you in the yard.
Do you remember? Then how she waned
in her bed as her blood turned
against her, unbidden mutation
that thieved her and left you
to wonder why? Consider how
you are your own reverse
leatherworker undoing the hide's taut
musculature. Again in: your lips
the vacuum tube of smog. But against
those odds, I wrecked you the most,
your baby—the only one, the one
you accepted but hadn't planned for—
who catalyzed your receding
gums, your brittling hair, who drains
the well of your charity through the years.
As soon as I began, you began
blanching despite your best efforts—
the vitamins, the dyes and creams,
and then the surgeries, each time
a mask, each mask a choice you made
that couldn't be worn forever. Exhale.
And even after all you've lived through,
you spend your days indignant, ashing
into your favorite bronze-glazed tray,
asking yourself why
no one stopped to warn you.

Tattoo as Echo, as Shade

If I wrote another something about my mother,
I'd turn her into my calf:
a blood sacrifice in black
and gray shades, ask the artist to dig

deep, press through the top layers
so the likeness wouldn't fade.
I'd ask for perfect symmetry except
the dark mole on her bottom lip, right side.

I wouldn't ask for stippled freckles.
Mine will show through after
the healing process ends. To say
this is my way to love her

would sound syrupy. Instead,
she is an excuse to subject myself
to the pleasure of the needle's bites,
thousands per minute,

gloved hands grabbing, pulling,
pushing my skin like a masseur's
slicked with dye, the Bactine spray
a reverse napalm soothing the burn,

the pulse—when he's all done—of my arteries
wrapped in plastic, blood compressed with ink.
And when I peel the wrap off hours later,
the wound almost sizzles in the rush of air.

My gasp, my geist, my phantom
pang I register but can't see
like how I hear my mother's voice
in the voices of most who call my name,

an echo, a shade. My continuous itch
to return and return asking the artist
not for something new but more of the same,
this measured pain I know, pain that awakens

a felt version of life that does not merely live
inside the confines of the brain, but in the buzz
of the gun as he starts up, the creak of his chair
as he leans over my limbs that reminds me

of the cracks of my mother's knees
as she'd rise from the couch after a long sit,
limp toward her potted plants to spill out
the dregs of her drinks. Such small offerings.

Asked why he insists on writing his mother's death:

He says he wants exposure.
     A sort of freedom—an awful growing into
not-having, an awful ringing.

He wants to be a sea warmed until it blooms
     with algae, its function
no longer its function and so it becomes

something separate, something new.
     How to know where to go except
imagining? Like a switch he presses.

He builds a cage for her.
     Her body is his stage.
She is a tumor he can slowly cut away

until he weighs only what *he* weighs, so light
     he can almost walk across the surface
of a lake. He becomes his own god

his own son his own mother.
     Or she is a honey-filled hive, a warm
house in which he can rest.

She rises like gas—sweet,
     sticky—and hangs there.
He inhales. She is the paint, the palette,

the easel, a Pollock-esque splattering so thick
     the canvas seems to wither under its own
immense gravity. His pen descends.

He burns her into his memory,
     spins her again and again
into another shimmering collapse

as if by making her glow he can somehow
        redeem himself for imagining her
in another minute as stone, shaped

then dynamited.
        He can't stop—
as if in stopping she would cease to be

anything at all. And so the next loop begins:
        he demolishes her then builds up
something other from the wreckage.

Matthew W. Baker grew up in Pittsburgh, PA but currently lives in Reno, NV and teaches middle and high school English. He received his MFA from the University of Nevada, Reno. His work has appeared or will appear in *The Summerset Review, The Matador Review, Booth Journal, Sundog Lit, Yemassee Journal, The Meadow*, among others, and has been nominated for the Best New Poets anthology. He can be found on Twitter at @mmbakes and Instagram at @emembakes.

www.ingramcontent.com/pod-product-compliance
Lightning Source LLC
LaVergne TN
LVHW021125080426
835510LV00021B/3322